AFRICAN WRITERS

Founding editor

PETER ABRAHAMS
6 *Mine Boy*

CHINUA ACHEBE
1 *Things Fall Apart*
3 *No Longer at Ease*
16 *Arrow of God*
31 *A Man of the People*
100 *Girls at War**
120 *Beware Soul Brother*†

TEWFIK AL-HAKIM
117 *Fate of a Cockroach*‡

T. M. ALUKO
11 *One Man, One Machet*
30 *One Man, One Wife*
32 *Kinsman and Foreman*
70 *Chief, the Honourable Minister*
130 *His Worshipful Majesty*

ELECHI AMADI
25 *The Concubine*
44 *The Great Ponds*
140 *Sunset in Biafra* §

JARED ANGIRA
111 *Silent Voices*†

I. N. C. ANIEBO
148 *The Anonymity of Sacrifice*

AYI KWEI ARMAH
43 *The Beautyful Ones Are Not Yet Born*
154 *Fragments*
155 *Why Are We So Blest?*

BEDIAKO ASARE
59 *Rebel*

KOFI AWOONOR
108 *This Earth, My Brother*

FRANCIS BEBEY
86 *Agatha Moudio's Son*

MONGO BETI
13 *Mission to Kala*
77 *King Lazarus*
88 *The Poor Christ of Bomba*

OKOT p'BITEK
147 *The Horn of My Love*†

DENNIS BRUTUS
46 *Letters to Martha*†
115 *A Simple Lust*†

SYL CHENEY-COKER
126 *Concerto for an Exile*†

DRISS CHRAIBI
79 *Heirs to the Past*

J. P. CLARK
50 *America, Their America* §

WILLIAM CONTON
12 *The African*

Keys to Signs

Novels are unmarked
*Short Stories
†Poetry
‡Plays
§Autobiography or Biography

BERNARD B. DADIÉ
87 *Climbié*

DANIACHEW WORKU
125 *The Thirteenth Sun*

MODIKWE DIKOBE
124 *The Marabi Dance*

MBELLA SONNE DIPOKO
57 *Because of Women*
82 *A Few Nights and Days*
107 *Black and White in Love*†

AMU DJOLETO
41 *The Strange Man*
161 *Money Galore*

CYPRIAN EKWENSI
2 *Burning Grass*
5 *People of the City*
19 *Lokotown**
84 *Beautiful Feathers*
146 *Jagua Nana*

OLAUDAH EQUIANO
10 *Equiano's Travels* §

MALICK FALL
144 *The Wound*

NURUDDIN FARAH
80 *From a Crooked Rib*

MUGO GATHERU
20 *Child of Two Worlds*

JOE DE GRAFT
166 *Beneath the Jazz and Brass*†

BESSIE HEAD
101 *Maru*
149 *A Question of Power*

LUIS BERNARDO HONWANA
60 *We Killed Mangy-Dog**

SONALLAH IBRAHIM
95 *The Smell of It**

OBOTUNDE IJIMERE
18 *The Imprisonment of Obatala*‡

AUBREY KACHINGWE
24 *No Easy Task*

SAMUEL KAHIGA
158 *The Girl from Abroad*

CHEIKH HAMIDOU KANE
119 *Ambiguous Adventure*

KENNETH KAUNDA
4 *Zambia Shall Be Free* §

LEGSON KAYIRA
162 *The Detainee*

A. W. KAYPER-MENSAH
157 *The Drummer in Our Time*†

ASARE KONADU
40 *A Woman in her Prime*
55 *Ordained by the Oracle*

DURO LADIPO
65 *Three Yoruba Plays*‡

ALEX LA GUMA
35 *A Walk in the Night**
110 *In the Fog of the Season's End*
152 *The Stone Country*

DORIS LESSING
131 *The Grass is Singing*

TABAN LO LIYONG
69 *Fixions**
74 *Eating Chiefs**
90 *Frantz Fanon's Uneven Ribs*†
116 *Another Nigger Dead*†

BONNIE LUBEGA
105 *The Outcasts*

YULISA AMADU MADDY
89 *Obasai* ‡
137 *No Past, No Present, No Future*

NAGUIB MAHFOUZ
151 *Midaq Alley*

NELSON MANDELA
123 *No Easy Walk to Freedom* §

RENÉ MARAN
135 *Batouala*

ALI A. MAZRUI
97 *The Trial of Christopher Okigbo*

TOM MBOYA
81 *The Challenge of Nationhood (Speeches)*

S. O. MEZU
113 *Behind the Rising Sun*

HAM MUKASA
133 *Apolo Kagwa Discovers Britain*

DOMINIC MULAISHO
98 *The Tongue of the Dumb*

JOHN MUNONYE
21 The Only Son
45 Obi
94 Oil Man of Obange
121 A Wreath for the Maidens
153 A Dancer of Fortune

MARTHA MVUNGI
159 Three Solid Stones*

MEJA MWANGI
143 Kill Me Quick
145 Carcase for Hounds

GEORGE SIMEON MWASE
160 Strike a Blow and Die §

NGUGI WA THIONG'O
7 Weep Not Child
17 The River Between
36 A Grain of Wheat
51 The Black Hermit ‡
150 Secret Lives*

ARTHUR NORTJE
141 Dead Roots†

NKEM NWANKWO
67 Danda

FLORA NWAPA
26 Efuru
56 Idu

ONUORA NZEKWU
85 Wand of Noble Wood
91 Blade Among the Boys

OGINGA ODINGA
38 Not Yet Uhuru §

GABRIEL OKARA
68 The Voice

CHRISTOPHER OKIGBO
62 Labyrinths†

KOLE OMOTOSO
102 The Edifice
122 The Combat

SEMBÈNE OUSMANE
63 God's Bits of Wood
92 The Money-Order with White Genesis
142 Tribal Scars*

YAMBO OUOLOGUEM
99 Bound to Violence

MARTIN OWUSU
138 The Sudden Return‡

FERDINAND OYONO
29 Houseboy
39 The Old Man and the Medal

PETER K. PALANGYO
53 Dying in the Sun

LENRIE PETERS
22 The Second Round
37 Satellites†
103 Katchikali†

JEAN-JOSEPH RABÉARIVELO
167 Translations from the Night†

MWANGI RUHENI
139 The Future Leaders
156 The Minister's Daughter

TAYEB SALIH
47 The Wedding of Zein*
66 Season of Migration to the North

STANLAKE SAMKANGE
33 On Trial for my Country

KOBINA SEKYI
136 The Blinkards‡

SAHLE SELLASSIE
52 The Afersata
163 Warrior King

FRANCIS SELORMEY
27 The Narrow Path

L. S. SENGHOR
71 Nocturnes†

ROBERT SERUMAGA
54 Return to the Shadows

WOLE SOYINKA
76 The Interpreters

TCHICAYA U TAM'SI
72 Selected Poems†

CAN THEMBA
104 The Will to Die*

REMS NNA UMEASIEGBU
61 The Way We Lived*

LAWRENCE VAMBE
112 An Ill-Fated People §

D. M. ZWELONKE
128 Robben Island

COLLECTIONS OF STORIES AND PROSE
9 Modern African Prose
Edited by Richard Rive
114 Quartet
By Richard Rive, Alex La Guma, Alf Wannenburgh and James Matthews
15 Origin East Africa
Edited by David Cook
23 The Origin of Life and Death
Edited by Ulli Beier
48 Not Even God is Ripe Enough
Edited by Bakare Gbadamosi and Ulli Beier
58 Political Spider
Edited by Ulli Beier
73 North African Writing
Translated by Len Ortzen
75 Myths and Legends of the Swahili
Edited by Jan Knappert
83 Myths and Legends of the Congo
Edited by Jan Knappert

109 Onitsha Market Literature
Edited by E. N. Obiechina
118 Amadu's Bundle
Malum Amadu
Edited by Gulla Kell and Ronald Moody
132 Two Centuries of African English
Edited by Lalage Bown

ANTHOLOGIES OF POETRY
8 A Book of African Verse
Edited by John Reed and Clive Wake
42 Poems from Ghana
Edited by Kofi Awoonor and G. Adali-Mortty
64 Seven South African Poets
Edited by Cosmo Pieterse
93 A Choice of Flowers
Translated by Jan Knappert
96 Poems from East Africa
Edited by David Cook and David Rubadiri
106 French African Verse
Translated by John Reed and Clive Wake
129 Igbo Traditional Verse
Edited by Romanus Egudu and Donatus Nwoga
164 Black Poets in South Africa
Edited by Robert Royston

COLLECTIONS OF PLAYS
28 Short East African Plays
Edited by David Cook and David Rubadiri
34 Ten One-Act Plays
Edited by Cosmo Pieterse
78 Short African Plays
Edited by Cosmo Pieterse
114 Five African Plays
Edited by Cosmo Pieterse
127 Nine African Plays for Radio
Edited by Cosmo Pieterse and Gwyneth Henderson
134 African Theatre
Edited by Gwyneth Henderson
165 African Plays for Playing
Edited by Michael Etherton

AFRICAN WRITERS SERIES

167

*Translations
from
the Night*

TRANSLATIONS FROM THE NIGHT

Selected Poems of
JEAN-JOSEPH RABEARIVELO

Edited with English translations
by John Reed & Clive Wake

LONDON
HEINEMANN
NAIROBI IBADAN LUSAKA

Heinemann Educational Books Ltd
48 Charles Street, London W1X 8AH
P.M.B. 5205, Ibadan · P.O. BOX 45314, Nairobi
P.O. BOX 3966, Lusaka

EDINBURGH MELBOURNE AUCKLAND
TORONTO HONG KONG SINGAPORE
KUALA LUMPUR NEW DELHI

ISBN 0 435 90167 2

Printed in Great Britain by
Cox & Wyman Ltd,
London, Fakenham and Reading

ACKNOWLEDGEMENTS

The editors would like to thank J.-J. Rabearivelo's literary executors, Solofo Rabearivelo and Jacques Rabemananjara, for permission to publish the poems and translations included in this volume. They would also like to thank the Reverend Alan Rogers for his help with the translation of the poem *Misy eritreritra atopatopanalina* (*There is a thought in the night tossed and tumbled*).

CONTENTS

Misy eritreritra atopatopanalina   2

SYLVES (1927)
Influences   6
Postlude   8

VOLUMES (1928)
Zahana   10
Filao   12

PRESQUE-SONGES (1934)
Lire   14
Naissance du Jour   16
Autre Naissance du Jour   18
Une Autre   20
Flûtistes   22
Haute Futaie   26
Zébu   32
Valiha   36

TRADUIT DE LA NUIT (1935)
Une étoile pourpre . . .   38
Quel rat invisible . . .   38
La peau de la vache noire est tendue . . .   40
Ce qui se passe sous la terre . . .   42
Un oiseau sans couleur et sans nom . . .   42
Les ruches secrètes sont alignés . . .   44
Te violà . . .   44
Toutes les saisons sont abolies . . .   46
Voici . . .   46
Il est des mains rouillées sans nombre . . .   48
Le vitrier nègre . . .   48

CONTENTS

Introduction   xiii

Bibliography   xxi

There is a thought in the night tossed and tumbled   3

SYLVES (1927)

Influences   7

Postlude   9

VOLUMES (1928)

Zahana   11

Filao   13

NEAR-DREAMS (1934)

Read   15

Daybreak   17

Another Daybreak   19

Another   21

Flute Players   23

Tall Timber   27

Zebu   33

Valiha   37

TRANSLATIONS FROM THE NIGHT (1935)

A purple star . . .   39

What invisible rat . . .   39

The hide of the black cow is stretched . . .   41

What goes on under the ground . . .   43

A bird that has no colour and no name . . .   43

The secret lives are drawn up . . .   45

There . . .   45

All seasons are repealed . . .   47

She is . . .   47

Blighted hands without number . . .   49

The glass-maker is a blackman . . .   49

Tu viens de relire Virgile . . .   50

Il y aura un jour, un jeune poète . . .   52

Celle qui naquit avant le lumière . . .   52

Lente . . .   54

Tu t'es construite une tour sous le vent . . .   56

Soeurs du silence en la tristesse . . .   56

Ecoute les filles de la pluie . . .   58

Il est une eau vive . . .   60

Vaines, toutes ces anticipations . . .   62

VIEILLES CHANSONS DES PAYS D'IMERINA (1939)

Dites, ô jeunes soeurs . . .   64

– Qui va là?   64

Pauvres nénuphars bleus . . .   66

Se couvre, se courvre le temps . . .   66

Là-bas, quelque part, vit la Grande-Soeur . . .   68

Là, si près, au nord . . .   68

– Abaissez-vous, abaissez-vous, ô collines . . .   68

– Puis-je entrer? Puis-je entrer? . . .   70

Par là, au nord, se trouvent deux pierres . . .   70

L'épouse est comme une feuille d'herbe . . .   70

– A-t-il enfin les ailes brisées, le Prince-libellule . . .   72

You have just re-read Virgil . . .   51
One day there will be a young poet . . .   53
She was born before the light . . .   53
Slow . . .   55
You built yourself a tower beneath the wind . . .   57
Sisters of silence in sadness . . .   57
Listen to the daughters of the rain . . .   59
There is a living water . . .   61
Vain, all those expectations . . .   63

OLD IMERINAN SONGS (1939)
Tell me, young sisters . . .   65
– Who is there? . . .   65
Poor blue water-lilies . . .   67
The sky clouds, clouds over . . .   67
Somewhere, over there, lives Big Sister . . .   69
Just over there, to the north . . .   69
– Down on your faces, hills . . .   69
– Can I come in? Can I come in? . . .   71
There in the north stand two stones . . .   71
A wife is like a blade of grass . . .   71
– Are his wings broken at last, the Dragonfly Prince . . .   73

INTRODUCTION

JOSEPH-CASIMIR RABEARIVELO (he later changed his first names to Jean-Joseph) was born in Antananarivo on the 4th March 1901, five years after Madagascar became a French colony. His mother was unmarried. Although she belonged to one of the noble families among the Hova people, the family wealth had been lost, and poverty followed the poet through his short life. As a child he attended Catholic mission schools though it was only later and through his own efforts that he acquired the full mastery of French which was to place him among the major black writers of the language.

The colonial society of Madagascar between the wars offered few opportunities for a career to a young Malagasy of intellectual ability. After trying various jobs, Rabearivelo worked from 1923 until the time of his death as a poorly paid proof-reader at the Imprimerie de l'Imerina. Naturally sensitive, conscious of his own powers and adopting the manner and pretensions of *fin de siècle* literary figures in Europe which became familiar to him through his reading, he found the humiliations of his status in colonial society hard to bear. In spite of – perhaps because of – the leading part he played in the intellectual life of Antananarivo, his friendship and collaboration with the French poet Pierre Camo, who was then living in Madagascar, and with Robert Boudry, Rabearivelo's life was one of continual frustrations and despair. He sought escape from this life and at the same time an identification with the style of life of many European poets of an earlier generation through alcohol, opium, gambling and promiscuity. In 1933 he wrote in his diary:

> Gambled like a lunatic until dawn. Drank like the sand the sea. By midnight I had lost every penny I had on me after a short run of luck . . . straight home to pick up all the ready cash we had, my wife and I, in the house . . . I lost it all again, it was the Chinese and the Indians who had me. Not home till 4.15 a.m., round and drunk as the moon. And so once more we have to start our life all over again.[1]

He was a voracious reader and, in an effort to break out of his colonial prison, he corresponded with writers all over the world. He was elated when he received replies but on the days when no letters came, more cast down than ever by his isolation: 'I am alone and depressed. There were no letters today. I feel abandoned, forgotten. I suffer dreadfully'.[2] He began to think of suicide and the idea seems to have taken stronger hold after the death of his favourite daughter Voahangy in 1933.

In 1937 his dream of visiting France seemed about to come true. Friends in the administration supported his application to join the Malagasy contingent at the Exposition Universelle in Paris that year. But Rabearivelo's request was refused and a group of basket-weavers sent instead. This disappointment seemed to have tipped the balance and on 22nd June 1937, after writing many letters and dispatching his manuscripts to various friends, he killed himself by taking cyanide. On 19th June he had recorded in his diary:

> The truth is I suffer and I suffer all the more because there is no one in whom I can confide completely. I would feel much less alone and my burden of solitude would not be as heavy as it is if at least, O God, I had the will to work.[3]

He wrote in his diary during the last few minutes of his life:

> No, it can't go on like this.
> And now, face to face with the Solitude that I go to create for myself, I cry out like Vigny's Moses, having been for more than 15 days (deliberately, it is true) without that drug which *widens what hath no bounds*.
> > I set my hand J.-J. Rabearivelo.
> > At the age of Guérin, at the age of Deubel
> > a little older than you, Rimbaud *anté-néant*.
> > > 22 June 1937,
> > > at 10.07[4]

Léon Deubel was a French poet who committed suicide in 1913 when he was thirty-four. His elaborately crafted sonnets were certainly an influence in Rabearivelo's early poetry and he may have read Deubel's letters which were published in 1931. Charles Guérin, also a poet, died at the same age as Deubel in 1907. Arthur Rimbaud was thirty-seven when he died in hospital after the amputation of a leg. He had recently returned from Africa where he had gone some years before in flight from the European literary world which Rabearivelo longed vainly to enter. The two lines which contain these names are the opening of a poem which Rabearivelo had written about his suicide shortly before. This self-dramatization, this mass of literary allusion are typical of Rabearivelo and the inauthenticity of so much of his life and death. Robert Boudry who knew the poet personally writes of him in *Jean-Joseph Rabearivelo et la mort* (p. 56):

It is clear that the western literature, the decaying Romanticism, the nebulous Symbolism, the black poetry,[5] existentialist before Existentialism, with which he was saturated as the body of a drunkard is saturated with alcohol, was 'rotting' him and his mind. Everything becomes for him allusions and quotations. Literature is for him not a pastime but the driving power of his brain and life, his reason for living. He saw in literature the means and the only possible means to escape from his situation as a Malagasy and from the island which he experienced as a prison. But literature did not bring him that oxygen, that hope that a young nation must have. It did not stir him to action but gave him instead a craving for the void and for despair.

Boudry's book, which is still the only extensive memoir on the poet and the main source of biographical information, takes the form of an investigation into the reasons for his suicide. Boudry concludes that Rabearivelo was killed by the narrowness and hypocrisy of the French colonial system. Yet it is necessary to note that this colonialism did not take the form of denying him education, of censoring the books he was allowed to read or refusing him the right to publish in his own country or elsewhere. If Rabearivelo had lived in Paris he could hardly have enjoyed a fuller or more productive literary life than he found in Antananarivo in the 1920s and 30s. He was actively involved with Pierre Camo's review *18° Latitude Sud* which ran from 1923 until 1927. It was in this that he published much of his early poetry. For a short period in 1930 and 1931 he and another Malagasy poet, R.-J. Allain, jointly edited their own review *Capricorne*. Besides the ranging literary discussions that were among his greatest pleasures, he reviewed the books of his French contemporaries, writing under the pseudonym of A. Valmond, and so kept in touch with developments in French poetry. The first volume of his own poetry, *La coupe de cendres*, was brought out by a publishing firm in Antananarivo in 1924. *Sylves* in 1927 and *Volumes* in 1928 were published by the Imprimerie de l'Imerina. Each of these volumes is a collection of poems in various traditional French forms, usually arranged in short sequences. We have chosen from this early work a few sonnets for this seems the form that Rabearivelo used most successfully. His techniques are those of the Symbolist poets, starting from Baudelaire who always remained for Rabearivelo the greatest poet of all. There is also the influence of the early Mallarmé, Heredia, Laforgue, Jammes and other poets deriving from these, writing after the turn of the century. These early poems of Rabearivelo's are conventional and imitative both in language and sentiment, but this is not to say that either in language or sentiment they are false. Rabearivelo's melancholy, his sense of exile, his deliberate, rather emblematic patriotism were shaped and even largely derived from his reading in French and other European poetry. This reading was assimilated and through the imagination becomes his true poetic self which in turn was able to develop into the fresh and far less derivative poetry which followed. Yet the literary personality and life-style which Rabearivelo derived from the study of the poets who influenced him, led him nowhere and in the end destroyed him. When Rabearivelo's own poetic voice is heard, as it is in the collections *Presque-songes* (1934), and more perfectly in *Traduit de la nuit* (1935), he has found his poetic subject, which is the play between the bright daylight of reality and the moonlight or darkness of the imagination. Most of his poems are concerned with the transition from one to the other – the twilight processes of dawn or dusk.

Unlike the Negritude poets who were beginning to write about the time of Rabearivelo's death, he had no programme, political or cultural. At the heart of Negritude there is the link between race and culture, whether this link is interpreted as the extension of the natural and physiologically based temperaments of certain races into cultural forms or as the historic experience of the race bringing forth racial self-consciousness to be the centre from which its valid culture unfolds. This link does not exist for Rabearivelo. Instead he begins from the disjunction, experienced in himself, between race and culture. In his journal he writes:

> It's no joke: a Latin among the Celts and with the features of a Celt – I say this with no wish to mock. Imagine reversing the roles and Jesus a European (origin, features etc.). And this is what I am: imperiously, violently, *naturally*, a Latin among the Melanians. And with the latters' features.[6]

The use of the terms 'Celt' and 'Melanian' indicates Rabearivelo's familiarity with Europe's attempts in the nineteenth century to found its imperial nationalism in theories of race. It was possible to derive the French nation from the Celtic stock or the Germanic, Frankish intermixture which gave the country its name. Yet the French language and arguably all French culture, derive from Latin, the language of a people quite separate from either of these racial groups. French culture is then itself an adoption, by racially distinct peoples, even at its source and centre, in France itself. That Rabearivelo's identification of himself as a Latin should be given in this terminology adds poignancy to his physical exclusion from the centres of French culture. Perhaps if, like Césaire and Senghor, he had been able to live and study in Paris he would have developed a form of Negritude parallel to theirs. As it was, his path, literary and personal, was very different.

It is true that Senghor, in his note on Rabearivelo who is included in the *Anthologie de la nouvelle poésie nègre et malgache*,[7] accepts him as a poet of black culture, expressing that culture through the medium of the French language. It is also true that Rabearivelo's work, taken as a whole, has many connections with Malagasy folk poetry and that Rabearivelo wrote in the Malagasy language, wrote on the traditional poetry of the Malagasy people and often celebrated in his poetry the soil and the landscapes of his native place. Yet the Malagasy elements seem always inside the elaborate personal utterance of a poet whose commitment to Latinity is complete. It is impossible to feel that Rabearivelo addressed himself to his own people or that he took upon himself as a conscious poetic task to interpret the Malagasy soul to the French-speaking world outside.

When *Presque-songes* first appeared, it was stated on the title page that the poems were 'traduits du Hova'. Boudry suggests that Rabearivelo added this to account for his abandonment of the traditional rhyming forms of his earlier verse, as if free verse poems would be acceptable if they were taken as translations. In fact the poet's move to free verse was probably occasioned by the rise of this form to dominance in metropolitan French poetry; and the style and imagination of *Presque-songes*, its vocabulary and images with the element of fantasy and childlike simplicity owe more to the work of Jules Supervielle, whose collection *Gravitations* was published in 1925, than to anything in traditional Hova poetry. The volume published in Antananarivo in 1960 and containing *Presque-songes* and *Traduit de la nuit* bears beneath the general title *Poèmes* 'traduit par l'auteur du Malgache'. It also contains Malagasy versions of all the poems, printed at the end of the book. There is however ample internal evidence to show that the French and not the Malagasy poems must be the originals.

Rabearivelo's more sensitive awareness of developments in contemporary French poetry coincided with his appreciation of the traditional Malagasy poetry known as the *hain-teny*, and he finally achieves in his mature poetry a genuine fusion of the two techniques. Since the beginning of his collaboration with Pierre Camo in *18° Latitude Sud*, Rabearivelo had from time to time published his own renderings of some of these traditional Malagasy poems. Sometimes he simply translated well-known poems, sometimes he altered or adapted them, sometimes he seems to have created original *hain-teny*. It is difficult for any but the expert to distinguish original from traditional elements. He published his *hain-teny* as prose, so that they resemble prose poems, a form which has become fashionable in French poetry since the Symbolists. Shortly before his death, he collected them together to make a volume, which was published posthumously by his friend Robert Boudry. It is with a selection from this volume, *Vieilles chansons des pays d'Imerina*, that our selection from Rabearivelo's poetry ends.

The presentation we have chosen suggests a steady progress from poetry which is French in form and atmosphere to poetry which is scarcely distinguishable from that of the Malagasy folk. Although this is a convenient way of arranging Rabearivelo's work for reading, it is a gross simplification of the progress of his poetic achievement. Rabearivelo's essay on Malagasy

[xviii]

poetry contributed to the Viennese journal *Anthropos* in 1923 shows that this interest came early and the *Vieilles chansons* though posthumously published do not belong particularly to the period between the publication of *Traduit de la nuit* and Rabearivelo's death.

Long before Rabearivelo began writing, the French author Jean Paulhan, who had spent some years teaching French in Madagascar and had learned to speak the Malagasy language, published a book on the *hain-teny*.[8] It appeared in 1913. Rabearivelo pays tribute to Paulhan's work on Malagasy folk poetry and he certainly knew his book. Paulhan records that while he was in Madagascar *hain-teny* were still current though they were despised by the younger generation, especially those receiving schooling, and he believed they would very quickly fall out of use except perhaps in the remoter villages. Paulhan's essay is in the form of an account of his own experience in trying to understand and to use the *hain-teny*, but the information which it contains can be summed up briefly. The word itself means 'language skill' or 'learned sayings'. The poems are gnomic, built up of proverbs and proverb-like phrases; each poem or section of a poem seems to conclude with a proverb in which its strength and significance lies. But at the same time the poems are enigmatic and deliberately obscure. The *hain-teny* is a dialogue or dispute, a little love-scene which may be a declaration of love, an acceptance or refusal of love offered, a lover's quarrel or a scene of parting. Paulhan tries to characterize the kind of love that occurs in the *hain-teny*. He calls it 'an intellectual, reasoning love, a love that discusses, and is more concerned to convince than to play on the feelings'. He points out that the Malagasy language does not distinguish sex grammatically, so that in many *hain-teny* it is not possible to tell which speaker is the man and which the woman and these poems can be read either way. But the most remarkable thing that Paulhan reports is the way the *hain-teny* were used. They were not recited for pleasure but employed as a method of conducting actual arguments in real life. Paulhan recounts a case he witnessed in which a dispute arose about the money due to a tiler who had just repaired the roof. The householder and the tiler adopted the roles of the disputing lovers in the *hain-teny* and conducted their altercation by means of these poems, one capping or answering the other until, in a way which Paulhan is unable to explain clearly, the tiler was defeated and had to accept the money offered.

The obscurity of the *hain-teny* is something familiar enough in modern poetry, although in his versions of these poems, Rabearivelo uses a naïve and sometimes archaic French unrelated to contemporary poetic idiom. He did not miss the similarity between these poems and the classical pastoral tradition. In his poem *Tu viens de relire Virgile* he shows how natural it was for him to conflate the reading of Virgil's *Eclogues* with the pastoral images of Imerinan life. No doubt, because of the way the *hain-teny* were used in Malagasy folk life, we should read the *Vieilles chansons* as we read Virgil's *Eclogues*, bearing in mind that these herdsmen and lovers with their country talk may also stand for other persons and other matters. The *Vieilles chansons*, the most Malagasy of Rabearivelo's work, are also the most Latin.

[1] As quoted by R. Boudry in his book *Jean-Joseph Rabearivelo et la mort*, p. 49. Rabearivelo's diary – which he entitled *Calepins bleus, temoins secrets, pythagoricques* – remains unpublished.

[2] Quoted by R. Boudry in his introduction to Rabearivelo's *Vieilles chansons des pays d'Imerina*, p. 14.

[3] R. Boudry: *Jean-Joseph Rabearivelo et la mort*, p. 79.

[4] Ibid., p. 80.

[5] Modishly morbid or sardonic poetry. The use of this term to refer to the poetry of Africans has become common only recently.

[6] R. Boudry: *Jean-Joseph Rabearivelo et la mort*, p. 80.

[7] Presses Universitaires de France, 1948. Re-issued 1969. Rabearivelo's poetry was also well represented in L. G. Damas' anthology, *Poètes d'expression française*, published by Seuil in 1947. The poems are preceded by a long biographical notice.

[8] *Les hain-teny*, P. Geuthner, Paris, 1913.

BIBLIOGRAPHY

POETRY

La coupe de cendres, Pitot de la Beaujardière, Antananarivo, 1924.

Sylves (*Nobles dédains, Fleurs mêlées, Destinées, Dixains, Sonnets et poèmes d'Iarive*), Imprimerie de l'Imerina, Antananarivo, 1927.

Volumes (*Vers le bonheur, La Guirlande de l'amitié, Interlude rythmique, Sept quatrains, Arbres, Au soleil estival, Coeur et ciel d'Iarive*), Impr. de l'Imerina, 1928.

Presque-songes (*traduits du Hova par l'auteur*), H. Vidalie, Antananarivo, 1934.

Traduit de la nuit (*poèmes traduits du Hova*), Ed. Mirages (Cahiers de Barbarie, publiés par les soins d'A. Guibert, no. 6), Tunis, 1935.

Chants pour Abéone, H. Vidalie, 1937.

Vieilles chansons des pays d'Imerina/précédées d'une biographie du poète malgache par Robert Boudry, Impr. Officielle, Antananarivo, 1939.

Des stances oubliées, Impr. Liva, Antananarivo, 1959.

Poèmes/Presque-songes/Traduit de la nuit (with a preface by J. Rabemananjara), Les Amis de Rabearivelo, Impr. Officielle, 1960.

24 Poems (translated from the French by G. Moore & U. Beier), Mbari, Ibadan, 1962.

Textes commentés by P. Valette, F. Nathan, Paris, 1967.

OTHER WORKS

Quelques poètes I/Enfants d'Orphée, The General Printing & Stationery Co. Ltd. (T. Esclapon), Port Louis, Mauritius, 1931.

Imaitsoanala, fille d'oiseau – cantate, Impr. Officielle, 1935.

Tananarive, ses quartiers, ses rues (with Eugène Baudin), Impr. de l'Imerina, 1937.

ARTICLES

'La poésie malgache', *Anthropos*, 1923.

'Notes sur la musique malgache', *Revue d'Afrique*, mai-juin 1931.

'La poésie malgache', *Revue d'Afrique*, avril-septembre 1933.

'Poésie et folklore malgaches', *Revue de Madagascar*, no. 28 janvier 1941.

Abasiekong, D. F.: 'Poetry Pure and Applied: Rabearivelo and Brutus', *Transition*, no. 23, vol. 5 no. 4, 1965.

Auber, J.: 'Jean-Joseph Rabearivelo (1901–1937)', *Revue de Madagascar*, no. 3, 3e trimestre 1958.

Beier, U.: 'Rabearivelo', *Black Orpheus* no. 11, n.d. (Reprinted in *Introduction to African Literature*, ed. U. Beier, Longmans, 1967.)

Boudry, R.: 'Jean-Joseph Rabearivelo et la mort', Présence Africaine, Paris, 1958.

'Jean-Joseph Rabearivelo', *Nouvelle Revue Française*, 1er septembre 1938.

'La mort tragique d'un poète', *Mercure de France*, 15 septembre 1938.

'Jean-Joseph Rabearivelo, poète malgache', *Revue de Madagascar*, janvier 1939.

Gérard, A. S.: 'Stèle pour un poète malgache', *Académie Royale des Sciences d'Outre-mer, Bulletin des Séances*, (2) 1968.

Guibert, A.: *Notre frère Rabearivelo*, Charlot, Algiers, 1941.

Razafintsambaina, G.: 'Hommage à Rabearivelo', *Présence Africaine*, no. 36, 1961.

Wake, C. & Reed, J.: 'Modern Malagasy Literature in French', *Books Abroad*, Winter 1964.

Wake, C.: 'Jean-Joseph Rabearivelo: a Poet before Negritude', in *The Critical Evaluation of African Literature*, ed. E. Wright, Heinemann Educational Books, 1973.

Misy eritreritra atopatopanalina

Misy eritreritra atopatopanalina
Vakivakim-botry tsy tafavoaky ny onja;
Misy eritreritra tsy afaka miarina
Ho tonga eo am-bava, fa ao anaty monja.

Vakivakim-botry tsy tody tora-pasika,
Mivalombalom-poana eo am-binanin-drano,
Jerena ny eo aloha, tany midadasika;
Ny eo aoriana kosa, rano be manganohano.

O ry eritreritro rebefa tera-bolana
ka toa misotro kintana izato zavatra hita!
O ry eritreritro mifatotra, miolana,
Vakivakim-botry mandeha fa tsy tafita!

Fotoana mamy loatra ny ahaterahanao,
Fa efa miala voly ery ampara-maso
izay rehetra inoantsika ho izao tontolo izao;
Dia ny tobin' ny eto Iarivo madio mangasohaso;

Fotoam-pahatoniana, fotoam-pahasambarana
Mety raha misandratra any anaty foko
Ny hira tsara indrindra, ny hira isay hamarana
Ny fara-vetsovetso, ny faran' ny toloko;

Kanefa re, kanefa ka zary tebiteby
No injao reko avy ao, tsy sahy mivoaka akory!
Dia tahotra sy hovitra no indro misomeby
Hovitra aman-tahotra no indro mifamory!

Tafihiny avy aoriana, reseny ny fotoana . . .
Hadino ny taloha, hadino ny ankehitriny;
Ny andro ho avy sisa no hita manoloana,
Ny ho avy manontany raha toa tsy hanan-tsiny.

[2]

There is a thought in the night tossed and tumbled

There is a thought in the night tossed and tumbled,
　A scrap of wreckage still sunk in the tide;
There is a thought too feeble to have stumbled
　Up to the lips, but lingers deep inside.

A scrap of wreckage not lodged on the beaches,
　In open water turning listlessly;
See there before it – the immense land reaches;
　See there behind – the vast and shining sea.

O thought of mine – born at the moon's rising
　That looming into sight drinks up the stars;
O thought of mine, knotted and agonizing,
　A scrap of wreckage as it restless fares.

The moon's birth is a time of ah! what sweetness,
　For then from weariness into our sight
Springs what we think the world in its completeness,
　Iarivo's suburb, clean and shining white.

A time of happiness, of consolation,
　A time when from my heart there rises high
My song of songs, to be the consummation
　Of my spilt words and all my bitter cry.

And yet – and yet – though it dare come no further,
　Deep down I hear a dread which has begun;
And fear and trembling work away together,
　Trembling and fear are now become as one,

And pounce on time behind – time is defeated,
　The present and the past are packing sent;
The days to come are in their places seated,
　The future asks, 'Can I stay innocent?'

　[3]

Inona? Eritreritra atopatopan' alina,
Vinakimbakim-botry mitady handresy onja
Inona? Eritreritra lavo tsy afa-miarina,
Tsy tonga teny akory, fa ao anaty monja!

Izao no bitsibitsiny, manaitra ny fanahy:
«Izahay no vakim-botry, ho tody sa ho very?»
Ny volana efa teraka. Ny saiko, io, manahy
Miparitaka, voazara, dia tonga very hery,

Zary tebiteby, zary fanahiana!
«Raha tonga hifampisolo ny ela sy ny ela,
«Inona re sisa no ampy mba hitoniana,
«Inona no ho voavonjy, inona no ho tavela?

«Fotoana mamy loatra no isainako an' izany
«Satria miala voly ery ampita manga
«Izay rehetra inoantsika no hany tena tany
«Dia ny tohin' ny eto Iarivo sy ny valan' ny eny Imanga»

What? A thought in the night tossed and tumbled,
    A scrap of wreckage struggling in the tide.
What? A thought collapsed, that has not stumbled
    Out into words but lies still slumped inside.

But there it murmurs – and the soul is shaken:
    'We are such scraps – we find a goal or drown.'
The moon has risen. Here my mind is taken
    By doubts, confused, divided, overthrown.

This is the dread, the ever-present worry:
    'What if the past always succeed the past?
What shall maintain its calm against Time's hurry?
    What shall be saved? What is there that can last?

And yet this thought still brings me ah! what sweetness,
    That still to light the dark horizon yields
What we think true, the world in its completeness,
    Iarivo's suburb and Imanga's fields.'

    Rabearivelo wrote this poem in *hova*. Found among his papers, it was published without a title at the end of *Poèmes* (1960).

Influences

Mon chant est imprégné de ta lumière vive
et son âme a subi, dès longtemps, l'influence
de la mobilité du son et des nuances
de ton horizon bleu, vaste ciel d'Iarive!

Mais que sa courbe épouse encore plus ta rive
beau fleuve auquel l'azur éternel se fiance
et sa souplesse aura la suprême élégance
de tes bords ténébreux que le soleil ravive,

afin d'honorer mieux cette langue étrangère
qui sait tant à mon âme intuitive plaire
et que j'adopte sans éprouver nul remords

quand j'apaise mon coeur sur les hautes terrasses
où, d'un regard ému, je dénombre les grâces
de ta beauté finie, ô terre de mes morts!

Influences

My song is saturated with thy light,
its soul so long has felt the influence,
Iarivo sky, encircling, blue, immense,
of all thy shifting shades of sound and sight.

But I would have my song's course wedded quite
to thine, fair river, sky-betrothed, that thence
its suppleness attain the elegance
of thy dim margins which the sun makes bright,

and I may honour more that foreign speech
which with delight my instinctive soul can reach,
which I adopt, nor grieve upon that head,

when from high terraces I soothe my heart
and, gazing moved, name over every part
of thy perfected grace, land of my dead.

Postlude

Souvenir, souvenir, automne de mon coeur,
quel oiseau chantera dans nos bois désolés,
et quelle floraison charmera la langueur
où, rois découronnés, nous sommes exilés?

Nos oiseaux les plus beaux, hélas! s'en sont allés,
et le Temps a tari, en sa lente rigueur,
la sève qui gonfle nos pampres mutilés,
nids où, souple et chantant, essaimait le bonheur!

Mais, en vain me contriste et m'alarme ton sort,
inéluctable fuite, inéluctable mort
de ma prime jeunesse au tournant de l'allée.

O souvenir: je sais quelle force de sang,
en les sombres débris obstinément celée,
te fait un éternel et bel adolescent!

Postlude

Memory, memory, autumn of my heart,
what bird will sing in woods deserted grown,
and what bright burst of flowers soothe the smart
where we are exiled, kings but overthrown?

The fairest of our birds, alas! are flown,
the sap that swelled our vines, now slashed apart,
harsh Time has dried; those nests where we have known
supple and singing joys in swarms upstart.

But yet in vain I mourn and dread your fate
for flight and death inevitably wait
for my first youth, there where the pathway turns.

O memory, I know beneath the drear
débris deep hid what strength of blood still burns
keeping you lad forever, fresh and fair!

Zahana

Ce n'est pas au jeu vain de nos vieux amoureux
qui s'écrivaient, jadis, sur tes feuilles naissantes
et, se rendant le soir en ton sein ténébreux,
saccageaient les rosiers sauvages de nos sentes,

ni même à la saveur de tes fruits succulents
où jutent les soleils de notre terre chaude,
que ton nom inconnu se doit d'être en mes chants
et d'y répandre tes purs frissons d'émeraude!

Mais, exilé des lieux d'où nous sommes natifs,
tu n'as plus dans nos champs que des jets maladifs
qu'une terre inclémente et stérile harasse!

Comme le mien ton front n'offre plus au matin
que les dernières fleurs d'un arbre qui s'éteint,
et ta défaite est soeur de celle de ma race!

Zahana

Not for those games that once our lovers played
when on your fresh-sprung leaves each wrote his name
and to the tryst at nightfall in your shade
plundered the wayside roses as he came;

nor for your fruit's sake, full of luscious savour
(our hot land's sunshine there to juice refines)
has your strange name in these my songs found favour
to send fine emerald tremors through my lines.

But after long exile from our native land
I see upon our fields your sad sticks stand,
I see a harsh soil wither them away.

Like me, at daybreak what have you to give
but the last flowers of trees that will not live:
your stock and mine being sisters in decay.

Filao

Filao, filao, frère de ma tristesse,
qui nous viens d'un pays lointain et maritime,
le sol imérinien a-t-il pour ta sveltesse
l'élément favorable à sa nature intime?

Tu sembles regretter les danses sur la plage
des filles de la mer, de la brise et du sable,
et tu revis en songe un matin sans orage
glorieux et fier de ta sève intarissable.

Maintenant que l'exil fait craquer ton écorce,
l'élan de tes rejets défaillants et sans force
ne dédie aux oiseaux qu'un reposoir sans ombre,

tel mon chant qui serait une oeuvre folle et vaine
si, né selon un rythme étranger et son nombre,
il ne vivait du sang qui coule dans mes veines!

Filao

Filao, brother of mine by sadness bound,
come to us from a far-off seaboard place,
what element in Imerinan ground
favours so inwardly your slender grace?

Sad for those dances on the beach you seem,
with daughters of the sea, the breeze, the sand,
you see some stormless morning in a dream
where proud in ever-surging sap you stand.

But now your exile mars you; your bark cracks,
your sprays once springing, now grown limp and lax,
grant but a shadeless refuge to the birds.

So were my song a thing of futile pains
if, born to foreign rhythms, measures, words,
it fed not on the blood that fills my veins.

Ne faites pas de bruit, ne parlez pas:
vont explorer une forêt les yeux, le coeur,
l'esprit, les songes . . .

Forêt secrète bien que palpable:
forêt.

Forêt bruissant de silence,
forêt où s'est évadé l'oiseau à prendre au piège,
l'oiseau à prendre au piège qu'on fera chanter
ou qu'on fera pleurer.

A qui l'on fera chanter, à qui l'on fera pleurer
le lieu de son éclosion.

Forêt. Oiseau.
Forêt secrète, oiseau caché
dans vos mains.

Read

Make no sound, do not speak:
off to explore a forest, eyes, heart,
mind, dreams . . .

Secret forest; yet you can touch this forest
with your hands.

Forest astir with stillness,
forest where the bird is gone, the bird to catch,
catch in a trap and make him sing
or make him cry.

Make him sing or make him cry
and tell the place where he was hatched.

Forest. Bird.
Secret forest, bird hidden
in your hands.

Naissance du Jour

Avez-vous déjà vu l'aube aller en maraude
au verger de la nuit?
La voici qui en revient
par les sentes de l'Est
envahies des glaïeuls en fleurs :
elle est tout entière maculée de lait
comme ces enfants élevés jadis par des génisses;
ses mains qui portent une torche
sont noires et bleues comme des lèvres de fille
mâchant des mûres.

S'échappent un à un et la précèdent
les oiseaux qu'elle a pris au piège.

Daybreak

Have you seen the dawn go poaching
in night's orchard?
See, she is coming back
down eastern pathways
overgrown with lilyblooms.
From head to foot she is splashed with milk
like those children the heifers suckled long ago.
She holds a torch in hands
stained black and blue like the lips of a girl
munching mulberries.

Escaping one by one there fly before her
the birds she has taken in her traps.

Autre Naissance du Jour

On ne sait si c'est de l'Est ou de l'Ouest
qu'est venu le premier appel;
mais maintenant,
dans leurs huttes transpercées par les étoiles
et les autres sagaies des ténèbres,
les coqs se dénombrent,
soufflent dans les conques marines
et se répondent de partout
jusqu'au retour de celui qui est allé dormir dans l'océan
et jusqu'à l'ascension de l'alouette
qui va à sa rencontre avec des chants
imbus de rosée.

Another Daybreak

Is it from the East or from the West
the first call comes? We do not know.
But now
in their huts transfixed by stars
and other assegais of the dark,
the cocks number off,
blowing into sea-shells,
answering on every side,
until the sleeper in the ocean comes again,
until the ascension of the lark
who goes to meet him and the songs she carries
are drenched in dew.

Une Autre

Fondues ensemble toutes les étoiles
dans le creuset du temps,
puis refroidies dans la mer
et sont devenues un bloc de pierre à facettes.
Lapidaire moribonde, la nuit,
y mettant tout son cœur
et tout le regret qu'elle a de ses meules
qui se désagrègent, se désagrègent
comme cendres au contact du vent,
taille amoureusement le prisme.

Mais c'est une stèle lumineuse
que l'artiste aura érigée sur sa tombe invisible.

Another

All the stars are melted together
in the crucible of time,
then cooled in the sea
and turned into a block of faceted stone.
A dying lapidist, the Night,
setting to work with all her heart
and all her grief to see her mills
crumbling, crumbling,
like ashes in the wind,
cuts with what loving care the prism.

The artist on her own unnoticed grave
sets up this monument of light.

Flûtistes

Ta flûte,
tu l'as taillée dans un tibia de taureau puissant,
et tu l'as polie sur les collines arides
flagellées de soleil;
sa flûte,
il l'a taillée dans un roseau tremblotant de brise,
et il l'a perforée au bord d'une eau courante
ivre de songes lunaires.

Vous en jouez ensemble au fond du soir,
comme pour retenir la pirogue sphérique
qui chavire aux rives du ciel;
comme pour la délivrer
de son sort;
mais vos plaintives incantations
sont-elles entendues des dieux du vent,
et de la terre, et de la forêt,
et du sable?

Ta flûte
tire un accent où se perçoit la marche d'un taureau
    furieux
qui court vers le désert
et en revient en courant
brûlé de soif et de faim,
mais abattu par la fatigue
au pied d'un arbre sans ombre,
ni fruits, ni feuilles.

Flute Players

Your flute,
cut from the thigh-bone of a mighty bull,
polished on the barren hill-sides
scourged by the sun.
His flute,
cut from the reed that quivers in the wind,
pierced on the banks of running water
drunken with moonlight dreams.

In the deeps of evening, you play them together
as if to right the sphered canoe
capsizing by the shores of sky
and keep it
from its doom.
But your plaintive incantations,
do they reach the wind gods
and the earth gods and the wood gods
and the gods of sand?

Your flute
draws out a note where the ear can catch the tread of a
    maddened bull
pounding toward the desert
and pounding back,
purnt by thirst and hunger,
felled by fatigue
at the foot of the tree without shadow,
without fruit, without leaves.

Sa flûte
est comme un roseau qui se plie
sous le poids d'un oiseau de passage –
non d'un oiseau pris par un enfant
et dont les plumes se dressent,
mais d'un oiseau séparé des siens
qui regarde sa propre ombre, pour se consoler,
sur l'eau courante.

Ta flûte
et la sienne –
elles regrettent leurs origines
dans les chants de vos peines.

His flute
is like a reed that bends
beneath the weight of a passing bird –
not a bird trapped by a child
ruffling its feathers,
but a bird lost from the flock
looking for comfort at his own reflection
in running water.

Your flute
and his –
longing for their past
in the songs of your grief.

Haute Futaie

Je ne viens pas pour saccager les fruits
que tu tends, sur tes cimes inaccessibles,
au peuple des étoiles et à la tribu des vents,
non plus pour arracher tes fleurs que je n'ai jamais vues,
dans le but de m'en vêtir ou d'en cacher quelque honte
    que j'ignore,
moi, l'enfant des collines arides.

Mais je me suis soudain souvenu dans mon dernier sommeil
qu'était toujours amarrée avec les lianes de la nuit
la vieille pirogue des fables
qui tous les jours faisait passer mon enfance
des rives du soir aux rives du matin,
du cap de la lune au cap du soleil.

Je l'ai ramée, et me voici en ton coeur, ô montagne
    végétale!
Me voici venu pour interroger ton silence absolu,
pour chercher le lieu où les vents éclosent
avant d'ouvrir des ailes trouées chez nous --
trouées par le filet immense des déserts
et par les pièges des villes habitées.

Qu'entends-je? que vois-je, ô haute futaie?
Voici des sons perdus qui se retrouvent et qui se perdent de
    nouveau
comme des fleuves souterrains
passés par d'énormes oiseaux aveugles
qu'emporte le courant rapide
pour être ensevelis sous la vase.

Tall Timber

I have not come to plunder the fruit
you offer on your inaccessible tops
to the people of the stars and the tribe of the winds,
nor to pick your flowers I have never seen,
to wear them or to cover some unconscious
    shame,
being myself a child of the barren hills.

But suddenly it came to me when last I slept
that the old canoe of fables
was still moored with creepers of night.
Every day it carried my childhood
from the shores of the evening to the shores of the morning,
from the headland of the moon to the headland of the sun.

I have paddled until I am here at your heart, plant-
    mountain!
I have come to question your absolute silence,
to find the nest where the winds are hatched
before spreading their wings that in our world are pierced,
pierced by the huge net of the deserts
and by the snares of peopled cities.

What do I hear, what do I see, tall timber?
Sounds that were lost are found and lost
    again
like underground rivers
crossed by enormous blind birds
carried away by the swift current
to be buried beneath the mud.

C'est ta respiration, ta respiration profonde
et déjà pénible comme celle d'un vieillard
qui gravit la côte de ses souvenirs
tout en descendant la pente des jours qui vont tarir.
Ta respiration, et celle de tes oiseaux innombrables,
et celle de tes branches broutées par tout un monde
    apocalyptique.

Mais que puis-je voir dans ta nuit sans couleur,
dans ta nuit plus éternelle que la mort des vertueux
et que la vie des misérables,
ô grotte de feuilles dont une issue se trouve peut-être au
    bord des mers
et l'autre dans l'abîme de l'horizon,
ô toi qui es pareille à un arc-en-ciel reliant deux continents?

Je ne verrai que le soleil qui se débat,
– comme un sanglier sagayé dans les buissons de l'azur –
sanglier de lumière pris dans les rets puissants
que tu tends au milieu de fruits mûrs et de fleurs durables,
là-haut, là-bas, à l'extrême limite
où le génie de la terre et la force de l'arbre peuvent se
    rencontrer.

Mais, plus tard, bien que des jours aussi innombrables
que tes feuilles successives soient déjà tombées dans l'éternité
bien que les nuits septuples aient plus de sept fois épaissi
    la nuit du temps,
tant que je pourrai cueillir les matins en fleurs
au bout de la tige brisée des soirs,
je garderai toujours le souvenir de ton silence et de ta
    clarté étranges.

It is your breathing, your deep breathing,
already painful like an old man's breathing
as he toils up the steep hill of his memories
and descends the slope of his days running out;
your breathing and the breathing of your innumerable birds
and of your branches browsed by a world of apocalyptic
    beasts.

What can I see in your colourless night,
in your night more lasting than the death of the good
and the lifetime of the wretched,
O cavern of leaves with a passage perhaps to the
    sea-shore
and another into the depths of the horizon,
you, like a rainbow linking two continents?

All I shall see is the sun floundering,
like a boar speared in the undergrowth of the sky,
boar of light taken in mighty nets
that you spread among ripe fruits and lasting flowers,
up there, down there, at the farthest limit
where the genius of the earth and the strength of the tree
    may meet.

But later, though days as beyond numbering
as the generations of your leaves have dropped into eternity,
though your sevenfold nights have more than seven times
    thickened the night of time,
so that I can pick the mornings flowering
at the end of the broken stalks of evening,
I will keep forever the memory of your strange brightness
    and silence.

Ils seront comme des galets projetés sur le sable
et ramassés par un vieux marin
qui les emporte chez lui et les place près de la coque
d'une minuscule pirogue à balancier
achetée dans une île lointaine que le rêve seul habite,
mais où des cabanes bordent la mer.

Ils seront plutôt comme des billes d'ébène,
de bois de rose ou d'autre essence précieuse
que je mettrai sur ma table
où ton souvenir les sculptera patiemment
pour en faire des fétiches aux yeux de verre,
des fétiches silencieux au milieu de mes livres.

They will be like pebbles thrown on the sand
and picked up by an old sailor
who takes them home and puts them beside the hull
of a miniature outrigged canoe
bought in some far-off island that only dreams inhabit,
but with huts lining the shore;

or better, like small logs of ebony,
of rosewood or some other precious stuff
that I shall lay upon my table;
patiently your memory will carve them
into idols with eyes of glass,
into idols keeping silent among my books.

Zébu

Voûté comme les cités d'Imerina
en évidence sur les collines
ou taillées à même les rochers ;
bossu comme les pignons
que la lune sculpte sur le sol,
voici le taureau puissant
pourpre comme la couleur de son sang.

Il a bu aux abords des fleuves,
il a brouté des cactus et des lilas ;
le voici accroupi devant du manioc
lourd encore du parfum de la terre,
et devant des pailles de riz
qui puent violemment le soleil et l'ombre.

Le soir a bêché partout
et il n'y a plus d'horizon.
Le taureau voit un désert qui s'étend
jusqu'aux frontières de la nuit.
Ses cornes sont comme un croissant
qui monte.

Désert, désert,
désert devant le taureau puissant
qui s'est égaré avec le soir
dans le royaume du silence,
qu'évoques-tu dans son demi-sommeil ?
Est-ce les siens qui n'ont pas de bosse
et qui sont rouges comme la poussière
que soulève leur passage,
eux, les maîtres des terres inhabitées ?
Ou ses aïeux qu'engraissaient les paysans
et qu'ils amenaient en ville, parés d'oranges mûres,
pour être abattus en l'honneur du Roi ?

Zebu

Domed like the villa   of Imerina
clustered on the hill-
or cut out of the rock
humped like the gabl
that the moon carves   the ground,
see the great bull
purple as the colour o   blood.

He has drunk at the e   of rivers,
he has cropped cactus   lilac;
now he crouches before   sava
still heavy with the sce   the earth,
before rice straw
fiercely reeking of sun a   hade.

Evening has trenched a   d
and the horizon has gon
The bull sees a desert th   aches
to the borders of night.
His horns are like a cresc
rising.

Desert, desert,
desert before the great bu
who is lost with the eveni
in the kingdom of silence,
what do you call to mind   s half sleep?
Those of his kind who hav   hump
and are red as the dust
their passing raises,
and who are masters of the   eopled lands?
Or his forefathers the peasa   attened
and led into towns, decked   ripe oranges,
to be felled in honour of the   g?

[33]

Il bondit, il mugit,
lui qui mourra sans gloire,
puis se rendort en attendant
et apparaît comme une bosse de la terre.

He leaps and he lows,
but he will die without pomp.
Meanwhile he turns back to sleep.
He looks like a hump of the earth.

Valiha

Blocs d'émeraude pointus
surgis du sol
parmi l'herbe dont le fleuve est cilié,
et ressemblant à d'innombrables cornes de jeunes taureaux
enterrés vivants par un clair de lune.

Il est une eau pure, il est une eau secrète,
froide comme le sable où elle se cache,
qui remplit ces frêles conques non perforées.

Puis deviennent une forêt de flûtes non travaillées,
deviennent un peuple de fûts
où de l'eau est captive depuis les origines :
deviennent des bambous bruissant de nids
et de vents.

Ils y résonneront
jusqu'à ce qu'y vienne un artiste
qui brisera leur jeunesse de dieux
et qui les écorchera dans sa cité
et tendra leur peau
avec des fragments de calebasses
et des bribes de lianes.

Et lorsque le soleil sera rouge,
lorsque les étoiles écloront
ou que les matins battront des ailes,
au bord de l'âtre
ou sur une natte neuve,
les bambous ne seront plus
que des choses chantantes
entre les mains des amoureux.

Valiha

Blocks of pointed emerald
spring from the ground
among the grass that fringes the river,
like the numberless horns of young bulls
buried alive one moonlit night.

A pure water, a secret water,
cold as the sand in which it hides,
fills these frail, unpierced shells.

Then they turn into a forest of unfashioned flutes,
a population of columns
where water has been prisoner since the beginnings,
turn into bamboos rustling with nests
and winds.

There they will sound
until an artist comes
who will break their godlike youth
and flay them in his village
and stretch out their skins
with shards of calabashes
and scraps of liana.

And when the sun is red,
when the stars unfold
or mornings clap their wings,
beside the hearth
or on a new mat,
the bamboos will be nothing
but things of song
between the hands of lovers.

Traduit de la nuit

Pour avoir mis le pied
Sur le coeur de la nuit
Je suis un homme pris
Dans les rets étoilés.

Jules Supervielle

I

Une étoile pourpre
évolue dans la profondeur du ciel –
quelle fleur de sang éclose en la prairie de la nuit –

Evolue, évolue,
puis devient comme un cerf-volant lâché par un enfant
endormi.

Paraît s'approcher et s'éloigner à la fois,
perd sa couleur comme une fleur près de tomber,
devient nuage, devient blanc, se réduit:
n'est plus qu'une pointe de diamant
striant le miroir bleu du zénith
où l'on voit déjà le leurre
glorieux du matin nubile.

II

Quel rat invisible,
venu des murs de la nuit,
grignote le gâteau lacté de la lune?
Demain matin,
quand il se sera enfui,
il aura là des traces de dents sanglantes.

Demain matin,
ceux qui se seront enivrés toute la nuit
et ceux qui sortiront du jeu,

[38]

Translations from the Night

Because I set foot
On the heart of the night
I am a man caught
In the starry nets.
　　　　Jules Supervielle

I

A purple star
turns in the depths of the sky –
a flower of blood unfolded in the prairie of night –

turns, turns,
until like a paper kite slipped from the hand of a child
　　asleep,

it seems at once to drift nearer and further away,
loses its colour like a flower ready to fall,
becomes a cloud, goes white, dwindles:
now it is only a diamond point
scoring the blue mirror of the zenith
where already the nubile morning sets
her splendid lure.

II

What invisible rat
out of the walls of the night
is gnawing at the milk-cake of the moon?
In the morning
he will be gone
and there will be the marks of bloodstained teeth.

In the morning
the all-night drinkers
and the gamblers, coming out,

en regardant la lune,
balbutieront ainsi:
'A qui est cette pièce de quat'sous
qui roule sur la table verte?'
'Ah! ajoutera l'un d'eux,
l'ami avait tout perdu
et s'est tué!'

Et tous ricaneront
et, titubant, tomberont.
La lune, elle, ne sera plus là:
le rat l'aura emportée dans son trou.

III

La peau de la vache noire est tendue,
tendue sans être mise à sécher,
tendue dans l'ombre septuple.

Mais qui a abattu la vache noire,
morte sans avoir mugi, morte sans avoir beuglé,
morte sans avoir été poursuivie
sur cette prairie fleurie d'étoiles?
La voici qui gît dans la moitié du ciel.

Tendue est la peau
sur la boîte de résonance du vent
que sculptent les esprits du sommeil.

Et le tambour est prêt
lorsque se couronnent de glaïeuls
les cornes du veau délivré
qui bondit
et broute les herbes des collines.

will look up at the moon,
muttering:
'Whose shilling is that
rolling across the green baize?'
'Ah!' one will say,
'our friend was skinned,
so he did himself in!'

And they all will snigger
and stagger and fall.
The moon, the moon will not be there:
the rat will have her, down his hole.

III

The hide of the black cow is stretched,
stretched but not set to dry,
stretched in the sevenfold shadow.

Who has felled the black cow,
dying without a low, dying without a roar,
dying without a chase
across the meadow flowered with stars?
Here she lies over half the sky;

stretched-out skin
over the sounding-box of the wind
carved by the spirits of sleep.

And the drum is ready
when the horns of the rescued calf
are crowned with lilies
and he leaps
and crops the grasses of the hills.

Il y résonnera,
et ses incantations deviendront rêves
jusqu'au moment où la vache noire ressuscitera,
blanche et rose,
devant un fleuve de lumière.

IV

Ce qui se passe sous la terre,
au nadir lointain?
Penche-toi près d'une fontaine,
près d'un fleuve
ou d'une source:
tu y verras la lune
tombée dans un trou,
et tu t'y verras toi-même,
lumineux et silencieux,
parmi les arbres sans racines,
et où viennent des oiseaux muets.

VI

Un oiseau sans couleur et sans nom
a replié les ailes
et blessé le seul oeil du ciel.

Il se pose sur un arbre sans tronc,
tout en feuilles
que nul vent ne fait frémir
et dont on ne cueille pas les fruits, les yeux ouverts.

Que couve-t-il?
quand il reprendra son vol,
ce sont des coqs qui en sortiront:
les coqs de tous les villages
qui auront vaincu et dispersé
ceux qui chantent dans les rêves
et qui se nourrissent d'astres.

[42]

There his cry will re-echo
and his incantations turn into dreams
until the time when the black cow rises,
white and pink,
before a river of light.

IV

What goes on under the ground
far down the deepest deep?
Lean over a fountain,
or a stream
or spring:
you will see the moon there
dropped down a hole
and yourself too,
gleaming, silent,
among trees that have no roots
and where songless birds come.

VI

A bird that has no colour and no name
has folded its wings
and pecked out the one eye of the sky.

It settles on a tree without a trunk
all in leaf,
that no wind sways;
its fruits are not to pick with open eyes.

What does it brood on in that nest?
When once again it takes its flight
what will come hatching out are cocks:
the cocks of all the villages
conquering and scattering
the cocks that crow in dreams
and feed on stars.

IX

Les ruches secrètes sont alignées
près des lianes du ciel,
parmi des nids lumineux.

Butinez-y, abeilles de mes pensées,
petites abeilles ailées de son
dans la nue enceinte de silence;
chargez-vous de propolis
parfumée d'astres et de vent:
nous en calfeutrerons toute fente
communiquant au tumulte de la vie.

Chargez-vous aussi de pollen stellaire
pour les prairies de la terre;
et demain, lorsque s'y noueront
les roses sauvages de mes poèmes,
nous aurons des cynorrhôdons aériens
et des semences sidérales.

X

Te voilà,
debout et nu!
Limon tu es et t'en souviens;
mais tu es en vérité l'enfant de cette ombre parturiante
qui se repaît de lactogène lunaire,
puis tu prends lentement la forme d'un fût
sur ce mur bas que franchissent les songes des fleurs
et le parfum de l'été en relâche.

Sentir, croire que des racines te poussent aux pieds
et courent et se tordent comme des serpents assoiffés
vers quelque source souterraine,
ou se rivent dans le sable
et déjà t'unissent à lui, toi, ô vivant,
arbre inconnu, arbre non identifié,
qui élabores des fruits que tu cueilleras toi-même.

[44]

IX

The secret hives are drawn up
near the lianas of the sky,
among the shining nests.

Go gathering, bees of my thoughts,
little bees winged with sound
in the cloud big with silence;
load up with bee-glue
smelling of stars and wind:
we will seal up every chink
that lets in the tumult of life.

Load up with star-pollen too
for the meadows of the earth;
and tomorrow, when come twining
my poems like dog-roses,
we shall have rose-hips of the skies
and seed-grain of stars.

X

There
standing naked,
clay you are and well remember;
but in truth you are child of this shadow in labour
fed fat with the moon's powdered milk,
then slowly you take the form of a shaft
on this low wall that the dreams of flowers climb over
and the scent of summer at ease.

To feel and believe that roots burst from your feet,
running and writhing like thirsty snakes
down to some underground spring,
or are clinched in the sand,
already made one with it, you living tree,
unknown, unnamed tree
who fashion fruit you will gather yourself.

[45]

Ta cime,
dans tes cheveux que le vent secoue,
cèle un nid d'oiseaux immatériels;
et lorsque tu viendras coucher dans mon lit
et que je te reconnaîtrai, ô mon frère errant,
ton contact, ton haleine et l'odeur de ta peau
susciteront des bruits d'ailes mystérieuses
jusqu'aux frontières du sommeil.

XIII

Toutes les saisons sont abolies
dans ces zones inexplorées,
qui occupent la moitié du monde
et la parent de floraisons inconnues
et de nul climat.

Poussée de sang végétal provisoire
dans un enchevêtrement de lianes ténébreuses
où est captif tout élan de branches vives.
Déroute d'oiseaux devenus étrangers
et ne reconnaissant plus leur nid,
puis heurts d'ailes – éclairs –
contre des rochers de brume
surgis du sol
qui n'est ni chaud ni froid
comme la peau de ceux qui s'étendent
loin de la vie et de la mort.

XIV

Voici
celle dont les yeux sont des prismes de sommeil
et dont les paupières sont lourdes de rêves,
celle dont les pieds sont enfoncés dans la mer
et dont les mains gluantes en sortent
pleines de coraux et de blocs de sel étincelants.

[46]

Your crest
hides in hair that the wind shakes
a nest of disembodied birds;
and when you come to sleep in my bed
and when I see it is you, my wandering brother,
your touch, your breath and the smell of your skin
will raise the rustle of mysterious wings
as far as the borders of sleep.

XIII

All seasons are repeared
in those unexplored regions
that make up half the world
and deck it with unknown blossoms
and no climate.

Thrust of provisory vegetable blood
in a tangle of shadowy lianas
where all the upsurge of living branches is trapped.
Bafflement of birds grown strangers,
no longer recognizing their own nests,
then wing-beats – lightning –
against rocks of mist
rising from the ground
that is neither hot nor cold
like the skin of those that lie
far from life and death.

XIV

She is
the one whose eyes are prisms of sleep,
whose eyelids are heavy with dreams.
Her feet are set deep in the sea,
her gluey hands reach out
full of coral and nuggets of sparkling salt.

Elle les mettra en petits tas près d'un golfe de brouillard
et les débitera à des marins nus
auxquels on a coupé la langue,
jusqu'à ce que tombe la pluie.

Elle ne sera plus alors visible,
et l'on ne verra plus
que sa chevelure dispersée par le vent;
comme une pelote d'algues qui se dévide
et peut-être aussi des grains de sel insipide.

XVI
Il est des mains rouillées sans nombre,
– ondes, ombres, fumées –
qui sarclent et marcottent
dans un buisson de framboisiers,
envahi d'herbes à hauteur de géant
d'où ne sortent que des oiseaux aveugles.

Que récoltent-elles, une fois lasses?
Qu'y aura-t-il entre leurs doigts de vent?
Des molles baies noires à force d'être rouges
sont déjà devenues d'innombrables champignons
au bord de ce fleuve sans piroguiers
pour embarquer tous ces paniers de fruits nocturnes.

XVII
Le vitrier nègre
dont nul n'a jamais vu les prunelles sans nombre
et jusqu'aux épaules de qui personne ne s'est encore haussé,
cet esclave tout paré de perles de verroterie,
qui est robuste comme Atlas
et qui porte les sept ciels sur sa tête
on dirait que le fleuve multiple des nuages va
    l'emporter,
le fleuve où son pagne est déjà mouillé.

[48]

She will set them down in little heaps beside a bay of mist
and dispense them to naked sailors
with their tongues cut out,
until the rain begins to fall.

By then she will be invisible,
and all we shall see
is her hair scattered by the wind
like a clew of seaweed unwinding,
and here and there perhaps a few grains of savourless salt.

XVI

Blighted hands without number
– billows, shadows, fumes –
that hoe and layer
in a raspberry thicket
weeds tall as giants have taken over,
where nothing emerges but blind birds.

What will they reap when they are weary?
What will they hold between their fingers of wind?
Soft berries reddened to blackness
have already become innumerable mushrooms
on the banks of that river where there are no canoe-men
to load all those baskets of nocturnal fruit.

XVII

The glass-maker is a blackman.
No one has ever seen his innumerable eyes,
no one has ever climbed to the height of his shoulders.
This slave tricked out with beads of glass
is as tough as Atlas
and carries the seven heavens on his head.
You would think that the manifold river of clouds would
    sweep him away,
the river in which his loin-cloth is already wet.

[49]

Mille et mille morceaux de vitre
tombent de ses mains
mais rebondissent vers son front
meurtri par les montagnes
où naissent les vents.

Et tu assistes à son supplice quotidien
et à son labeur sans fin;
tu assistes à son agonie de foudroyé
dès que retentissent aux murailles de l'Est
les conques marines –
mais tu n'éprouves plus de pitié pour lui
et ne te souviens même plus qu'il recommence à souffrir
chaque fois que chavire le soleil.

XVIII

Tu viens de relire Virgile,
tu viens aussi d'écouter les enfants
qui saluent la néoménie,
et les contes et les fables de ceux qui ne sont plus.

Est-ce l'heure bucolique,
ô coeur aspirant au repos,
coeur aussi hâlé que les roches?

Les pâtres? Ils ne sont pas ici;
leurs troupeaux? Regarde ces chèvres sauvages
aux cornes remplies de brume.
Leurs houlettes? voici que les arbres unissent leurs cimes.

Les pâtres sont là-bas, ils escaladent le ciel
il y a des herbes nouvelles sous leurs pas,
il y a des fruits irréels autour d'eux,
et des sources cachées qu'ils cherchent.

Thousands and thousands of splinters of glass
fall out of his hands
but bounce up back towards his forehead
battered by the mountains
where the winds are born.

And you are there at his daily torment,
his never-ending toil;
you are there when he is blasted and dying
every time the great conches resound
against the ramparts of the East.
But you have stopped pitying him
and do not even remember that his suffering begins again
each time the sun keels over.

XVIII

You have just re-read Virgil,
you have also just heard the children
greeting the new moon,
and the stories and fables of those who are no more.

Is it the pastoral hour,
O heart wooing rest,
heart tanned as rocks?

The herdsmen? They are not here.
Their flocks? See the wild goats,
their horns filled with mist.
Their crooks? See how the trees join together their tops.

The herdsmen are over there, they scale the sky.
There are new grasses beneath their steps,
there are unreal fruits around them,
and hidden springs that they seek.

Et toi, et toi, tu crois être Corydon
tandis que, devant toi, apparaît comme un Alexis
qui souffle dans les flûtes
que sont devenues toutes les branches.

XIX

Il y aura un jour, un jeune poète
qui réalisera ton voeu impossible
pour avoir connu tes livres
rares comme les fleurs souterraines,
tes livres écrits pour cent amis,
et non pour un, et non pour mille.

Sur le golfe d'ombre où il te relira
à la seule lueur de son coeur où rebattra le tien,
il ne te croira pas
dans les houles pacifiques
dont s'empliront toujours les abysses sans soleil,
ni dans le sable, ni dans la terre rouge,
ni sous les rochers dévorés de lichens
qui s'étendront derrière lui
jusqu'au pays des vivants
aveugles et sourds depuis la Genèse.
Il lèvera la tête
et pensera que c'est dans l'azur,
parmi les étoiles et les vents,
que ton tombeau aura été érigé.

XXI

Celle qui naquit avant la lumière,
est-ce aujourd'hui son septième jour,
aujourd'hui comme hier et comme en l'éternité
sans passé ni futur?

And you, you think of yourself as Corydon;
an Alexis appears before you
breathing into the flutes
which all the branches have become.

XIX

One day there will be a young poet
who will bring true your impossible wish
and come to know your books
as rare as flowers under the ground,
books written for a hundred friends,
not for thousands, not for one.

On the shadowy gulf where he will read you
by the sole light of his heart where yours now beats,
he will not think you are
in the pacific surges
that fill forever the sunless deep,
nor in the sand, nor in the red earth,
nor beneath the rocks eaten by lichen
which stretch behind him
to the land of the living
blind and deaf since Genesis.
He will raise his head
and think that in the sky
among the stars and winds
your tomb is built.

XXI

She was born before the light.
Is today her seventh day,
today as yesterday, as in eternity,
without past or future?

Elle renaît pourtant
avec le sommeil des oiseaux
et tandis que se cachent les pierres blanches
sur les sentiers qu'ont désertés les chèvres
comme sur les routes où court le silence.

Mais tu ne vois d'elle que ses myriades d'yeux,
ses yeux reptiliens et triangulaires
qui s'ouvrent un à un
entre les lianes célestes.

XXIII

Lente
comme une vache boiteuse
ou comme un taureau puissant
aux quatre jarrets coupés,
une grosse araignée noire sort de la terre
et grimpe sur les murs
puis s'arc-boute péniblement au-dessus des arbres,

jette des fils qu'emporte le vent,
tisse une toile qui touche au ciel,
et tend des rets à travers l'azur.

Où sont les oiseaux multicolores?
Où sont les chantres du soleil?
– Les lueurs jaillies de leurs yeux morts de sommeil
dans leurs escarpolettes de lianes,
font revivre leurs songes et leurs résonances
en cette évanescence de lucioles
qui devient une cohorte d'étoiles
pour déjouer l'arachnéenne embûche
que déchireront les cornes d'un veau bondissant.

Yet she is reborn
with the sleep of birds
while the white stones are hidden
on paths deserted by the goats
as on roads where silence runs.

But you see of her only her myriads of eyes,
her reptilian, triangular eyes
opening one by one
between the lianas of heaven.

XXIII

Slow
as a limping cow
or a mighty bull
four times houghed,
a great black spider comes out of the earth
and climbs up the walls
then painfully sets his back against the trees,

throws out his threads for the wind to carry,
weaves a web that reaches the sky
and spreads his nets across the blue.

Where are the many-coloured birds?
Where are the precentors of the sun?
– Lights burst from their sleep-deadened eyes
among their liana-swings,
reviving their dreams and their reverberations
in that shimmering of glow-worms
that becomes a cohort of stars,
and turns the spider's ambush
which the horns of a bounding calf will tear.

XXVI

Tu t'es construite une tour sous le vent
puis tu t'es accroupie sur l'eau,
ô reine sans visage
dont la pointe de la couronne
défie ce-qui-deviendra-pluies,
et dont les diamants embués
sont faits d'astres, et rien que d'astres.

O belle âme de ce-qui-change;
ô soeur et fille, tour à tour,
de cette lune qui vient de naître
à l'orée d'un verger,
tu as bâti sous le vent
et tu habites sur l'eau
comme mes rêves de sagesse!

Que nous fera la chute brusque
de ce qui est notre royaume?

Comme la tour, comme la mienne,
comme la perfide que foulent nos pieds,
cette joie dont pétille nos yeux,
si elle doit bientôt s'éteindre,
ne nous reviendra-t-elle pas autre et nouvelle?

XXVII

Soeurs du silence en la tristesse,
les fleurs qui n'ont que leur beauté
et leur solitude,
les fleurs – morceaux de coeur terrien
palpitant à l'unisson des nids –
dorment-elles ici, font-elles des rêves
sur la fin de leur destinée?

XXVI

You built yourself a tower beneath the wind,
you crouched upon the water,
O faceless queen.
The tip of your crown
defies the rains-to-be,
your clouded diamonds
are made of stars, nothing but stars.

Fair soul of all-that-changes,
sister and daughter turn by turn
of that moon just born
at the verge of an orchard,
you have built beneath the wind
and you dwell upon the water
like my dreams of wisdom.

What will it mean to us, the sudden fall
of that which is our kingdom?

Like the tower, like my own,
like the traitress our feet spurn,
that joy which sparkles in our eyes,
if it must so soon be quenched
will it not come again, changed and new?

XXVII

Sisters of silence in sadness,
flowers that have nothing but their beauty
and their loneliness,
flowers – fragments of the earth's heart
beating in unison with the nests –
are they sleeping here, are they dreaming
on the end that awaits them?

Les doigts
qui ne voulaient d'elles que leur jeunesse,
les doigts se sont tous joints
dans la chaude blancheur des draps –
sauf les miens qui sont si frêles
et qui savent tant choyer
les choses délicates.

Mes lèvres aussi frôlent les fleurs,
les fleurs devenues plus mystérieuses,
et plus belles, et brusquement hardies.

Et j'entends,
mêlées à la respiration des herbes,
leurs dernières confidences.
Ah! comme elles seraient douloureuses
sans ces parfums pacifiques, Seigneur,
qui s'évadent avec leur vie!

XXVIII

Ecoute les filles de la pluie
qui se poursuivent en chantant
et glissent
sur les radeaux d'argile
ou d'herbes de glaïeuls
qui couvrent les maisons des vivants.

Elles chantent,
et leurs chants sont si passionnés
qu'ils deviennent des sanglots
et se réduisent en confidences . . .
Peut-être pour mieux faire entendre
cet appel d'oiseau qui t'émeut.

Fingers
that wanted from them only their youth,
fingers all joined
in the hot whiteness of sheets –
except mine which are so frail
and can so cherish
delicate things.

My lips, too, brush the flowers,
flowers grown more mysterious,
and more lovely, and abruptly bold.

And I hear,
mingled with the breathing of the grass,
their last secrets.
Ah! how sorrowful they would be
without these perfumes of peace, Lord,
which fade away with their life!

XXVIII

Listen to the daughters of the rain,
chasing one another, singing,
slipping
on the rafts of clay
or the sword-grass blades
that cover the houses of the living.

They sing,
and their songs are so intense
they turn to sobs,
drop to murmur secrets . . .
perhaps to let you catch
the call of a bird that troubles you so.

Un oiseau seul au coeur de la nuit,
et il ne craint pas d'être ravi par les ondines?
O miracle! ô don inattendu!
Pourquoi rentres-tu si tard?
un autre a-t-il pris ton nid
tandis que tu étais en quête d'un rêve au bout du monde?

XXIX

Il est une eau vive
qui jaillit dans l'inconnu
mais qui mouille le vent
que tu bois,
et tu aspires à sa découverte
derrière ce roc massif
détaché de quelque astre sans nom.

Tu te penches,
et tes doigts caressent le sable.
Soudain tu repenses à ton enfance
et aux images qui l'ont charmée –
surtout à celle où ces mots naïfs mais étonnants se trouvaient:
LA VIERGE AUX SEPT DOULEURS:

Et voici une autre eau vive
qui ne cesse de sourdre sous tes yeux,
mais qui attise ta soif:
ton ombre
– l'ombre de tes rêves –
devient septuple
et, émergeant de toi,
alourdit la nuit déjà dense.

A solitary bird at the heart of the night,
not afraid that the nymphs will steal him away?
A miracle – an unexpected gift!
Why do you return so late?
Has someone taken your nest
while you were after a dream at the end of the world?

XXIX

There is a living water
springing in the unknown
but moistening the wind
you drink,
and you hope to discover it
behind that massive rock
broken from some nameless star.

You bend over it,
and you finger the sand.
All at once you think of your childhood
and the images that intrigued it –
especially the one with these simple but astounding words:
THE VIRGIN OF THE SEVEN SORROWS.

And here is another living water
that wells up continually from beneath your eyes,
but inflames your thirst:
your shadow
– the shadow of your dreams –
becomes sevenfold
and, escaping from you,
weighs down the night, already dense.

XXX

Vaines, toutes ces anticipations
qui veulent nous donner des ailes
et qui promettent
que nous séduirons un jour quelque Martienne?

Vain aussi, le rêve
qui perdit Icare
plus que le soleil
qui but la cire merveilleuse?

Mais quel triomphe certain
m'annoncent déjà tous ces signaux
que terre et ciel s'envoient
à l'orée du sommeil:

dans nos cités de vivants
jusqu'aux plus humbles huttes
répondent aux appels de feu
jaillis des étoiles naissantes.

XXX

Vain, all those expectations
that would grant us wings
and promise
one day some girl from Mars will fall for us?

Vain, too, the dream
that finished Icarus,
more than the sun
that sipped the marvellous wax?

But what confident triumph
already promised me by all those signals
exchanged between earth and sky
at the border of sleep:

in our villages of the living
even the humblest huts
give answer to those cries of fire
flashed from the new-born stars.

Dites, ô jeunes soeurs qui vous reposez à mi-chemin, là-bas, de cette montée: que vous a-t-elle dit à mon intention, la grande soeur, au pied de la côte?

— 'Je me suis baignée au moment du repiquage, a-t-elle dit pour le premier né, et ne pourrai venir comme les autres.'

— Ce sont là paroles d'une oublieuse déjà; mais de moi qui suis encore triste, cela ne peut être le message! Le riz lui-même est triste de la viande, ô jeunes soeurs; et moi, de penser à elle, m'ôte le sommeil! Depuis que je me suis séparé de cette femme mienne-là, comme je suis devenu fou au point de ne plus savoir compter: deux enfants deviennent trois, trois enfants deviennent deux! Comment parvenir au suprême renoncement?

— 'Mâchez, mâchez, a-t-elle dit, un bout de votre lambe; buvez, buvez de l'eau chaude; poussez, poussez un énorme bloc rocheux et allez au sommet du tombeau car c'est là que se cachent les cinq hommes qui ne se peuvent parler et les sept femmes qui se sont dépouillées de leurs parures!'

— Je vais délimiter ainsi la terre qui reviendra à cette femme: elle partira du Bois-Joli vers le sud, et de la Cité-des-Mille, vers le nord. Si plus tard j'avais cherché sans avoir rien trouvé et avais demandé sans avoir rien obtenu, je reviendrais encore deviser avec vous.

*

— Qui va là? Est-ce Celle-dont-les-pas-résonnent-des-jours entiers? Est-ce Celle-qu'il-est-difficile-d'interroger?

— Ce n'est ni Celle-dont-les-pas-résonnent-des-jours-entiers, ni Celle-qu'il-est-difficile-d'interroger! Mais je suis la femme d'un autre, et des jours entiers je dois être soumise! Je suis aussi la femme d'un autre, et je n'aime pas trop qu'on me parle de nos secrets! Plantez donc un pied de figuier: peut-être son ombrage me ferait-il venir! Plantez des pieds de ricin: peut-

[64]

Tell me, young sisters, resting there halfway on your climb, what message did she give you for me, the big sister, at the foot of the hill?

– 'I bathed at the time of the rice-planting,' was her message for the first-born. 'I shall not be able to come like the others.'

– Those are the words of a woman who has forgotten already. But I am a man still full of sadness; that cannot be the message I send! The rice itself is full of sadness for the meat, young sisters; and for me, thinking of her has taken away my sleep. Since I was parted from that woman of mine, I have grown so stupid I have forgotten how to count – two children become three, three children two! How can I bring myself to give her up forever?

– 'Chew,' she said, 'chew on an end of your lamba; drink, drink up hot water; push, push a huge boulder and go up to the top of the tomb for it is there are hidden the five men who cannot speak to each other and the seven women who have stripped off their fine clothes!'

– This is how I am going to lay down what land is to come to this woman: it will stretch from Fair-Wood southwards and from the Village-of-the-Thousand northwards. Later if I had searched and found nothing, asked and received nothing, I would come back and talk with you again.

*

– Who is there? Is it the Woman-whose-footsteps-echo-the-livelong-days? Is it the Woman-who-is-hard-to-question?

– It is not the Woman-whose-footsteps-echo-the-livelong-days nor the Woman-who-is-hard-to-question! But I am the wife of another, and the livelong days I must know my place. Besides I am the wife of another, and when someone tells me our secrets I am not at all pleased. So plant one root of fig-tree: perhaps its shadow would make me come. Plant a few roots of

être parviendriez-vous à me retenir! Plus me plaît de longue-
ment marcher avant d'avoir la cruche pleine, que d'emporter
tout de suite une cruche à moitié vide!

– Si vous m'offrez des fruits verts, je vous en proposerai qui
sont amers!

*

Pauvres nénuphars bleus: toute l'année ils ont des larmes
jusqu'au cou! Brins d'herbes d'eaux, brins de joncs de mares
charriés par les pirogues, abritez-moi: je suis si malheureuse!
Volez pour moi un peu d'amour: je suis à un autre! Votre
femme, aimez-la; moi, ne m'abandonnez pas! Qui n'a pas de
piment, il n'éprouve pas de volupté en mangeant; qui a perdu
son piège à poissons n'aura pas de friture. Et moi, si je vous
perds, je perdrai mon plus proche parent!

*

Se couvre, se couvre le temps mais ne se décide pas à
pleuvoir. Un véritable printemps de famille. Je suis la plus
belle étoile de la Constellation, et ce, grâce à l'amitié des
autres. S'appelle-t-elle toujours La-Belle-qui-rend-heureux,
celle à qui l'on m'a fiancé dans mon enfance? Elle apprenait,
en ce temps-là, à marcher, était facile à soigner, ne se plaignait
d'aucune blessure et ne pensait pas à me donner de rival.
Couchée, personne ne passait par-dessus son corps; personne
ne songeait à la sortir du sommeil. Elle était comparable à un
martin-pêcheur mâle qui rase l'eau: beaux reflets bleus.

Me croiriez-vous maintenant un pèlerin affamé dans le
désert et réduit à cueillir de maigres feuilles dans les fossés?
Croiriez-vous que le riz de mon silo fût épuisé et que je fusse
obligé de faire cuire des grains mêlés de cailloux? Croiriez-
vous qu'il n'y a plus pour moi de belles à choisir dans le village
et que bientôt l'on me verrait à la poursuite d'une femme non
consentante? Oui! me prendriez-vous pour une sauterelle
bleue ou verte, que je fusse à la merci de n'importe qui a des
doigts?

[66]

castor-oil tree: perhaps then you might be able to hold me. I would rather walk a long way to get my pitcher filled than take away a half empty pitcher with no waiting!

– Offer me green fruits and I will offer you bitter ones.

*

Poor blue water-lilies: the whole year long they have tears up to the neck! Grass blades of the waters, rush blades of the pools, driven by the canoes, shelter me: I am so wretched! Steal a little love for me: I belong to someone else! Your wife, love her; but do not leave me! Without allspice, no pleasure in eating. When the fish-trap is lost there is nothing to fry. If I lose you, I lose my closest kinsman.

*

The sky clouds, clouds over but cannot make up its mind to rain. Quite the family springtime! I am the finest star in the Constellation and that is thanks to the friendship of others. Is she still called the Fair-one-who-makes-happy, the woman they engaged me to marry when I was a child? That was the time she was learning to walk, was easy to look after, never cried when she hurt herself, never dreamt of giving me a rival. When she was asleep, no one stepped over her, no one dreamed of waking her up. She was like a cock kingfisher skimming the water: beautiful blue reflections.

Perhaps you would think that now I am a pilgrim starving in the desert, reduced to collecting scanty leaves in the ditches? Perhaps you would think that the rice in my silo was used up and I was forced to cook grain mixed with gravel? Perhaps you would think there are no more girls for me to choose from in the village and that soon you will see me running after a woman who does not want me? Yes! Perhaps you would take me for a blue or green grasshopper, at the mercy of anyone with fingers?

Non! je ne suis pas comme cette bande épaisse de criquets qui vient de loin et qui s'abat n'importe où et à tout moment!

Poils se trouvant sur la tête du ver à soie métamorphosé, vous avez le choix entre rester et partir.

*

Là-bas, quelque part, vit la Grande-Soeur. Elle est seule chez elle. Belle elle est l'hiver, splendide en été et luisante au printemps: nulle saison ne la trouve fanée, aucune demi-journée. Elle ne marche jamais le soleil sec, et ne sort jamais qu'au soir commençant. Elle ne se baigne jamais avec l'eau des cruches, mais toujours avec celle des yeux.

*

Là, si près, au nord, il y avait deux oranges jumelles: l'une était mûre, et l'autre belle à rendre heureux. J'ai donné la mûre à la Chère, et la belle à rendre heureux à l'Aimée. Mais j'ai beau chérir l'une et vraiment aimer l'autre, si elles me voulaient trop violemment dompter, je n'en saurais que faire.

*

— Abaissez-vous, abaissez-vous, ô collines, là-bas, à l'ouest, que je puisse voir de loin ces perles de corail enfilées, ces perles d'étain fondues! Est-il fondu, ce que vous aviez au coeur, Madame, pour que se fonde ce que j'ai au ventre? Ce lambe mien-ci, je ne permettrai jamais à l'eau de l'emporter; je ne le battrai jamais contre la pierre.

— Qui refuserait de mourir? Seuls ceux qui n'ont pas d'amour sont vaincus.

*

No, I am not like the thick swarm of crickets that comes from far away and drops down anywhere, at any time.

Hairs on the head of the silkworm after its metamorphosis; you can choose between staying and going.

*

Somewhere, over there, lives Big Sister. She lives by herself. Beautiful in winter, splendid in summer, radiant in the spring: no season finds her drooping even for half a day. She never walks in the sun and never goes out except at the beginning of the evening. She never washes in water from a pitcher, always with water from her eyes.

*

Just over there, to the north, there were a pair of oranges: one was ripe and the other fair enough to make you happy. I gave the ripe one to my Darling and the one fair enough to make you happy to my Beloved. But what is the use of loving one dearly and being really in love with the other? If they both grew too keen to bring me to heel, I would not know what to do.

*

– Down on your faces, hills, over there to the west, lie down, so that I can see, far off, those pearls of threaded coral, those pearls of smelted tin. Has what you have in your heart melted, my lady, so that what I have in my belly may melt? My lamba, I shall never let the water carry it off; I will never beat it against the rock.

– Who would refuse to die? Only those who have no love are conquered.

*

— Puis-je entrer? Puis-je entrer?

— Qui est là? Qui est là?

— C'est moi, le premier-né de mon père et de ma mère.

— C'est le premier-né de son père et de sa mère? Celui qui a des vêtements aux belles couleurs et qui porte haut la tête? Celui qui sautille sur ses souliers et va se poser dans son palanquin? Alors, entrez, jeune homme: le petit veau est bien attaché, et mon père et ma mère sont partis loin! Pourtant, si vous désirez voir un pagne aussi fin qu'ailes de sauterelle ou de libellule, allez ailleurs! Si vous venez aussi pour d'éphémères regrets d'amour, je préfère renoncer à vous avant que de vous avoir!

*

Par là, au nord, se trouvent deux pierres qui se ressemblent un peu: l'une est noire, l'autre blanche. Si je pince la blanche, j'ai honte de la noire; si je pince la noire, j'ai honte de la blanche; si je les pince toutes deux, l'une est amour, l'autre consolation.

*

L'épouse est comme une feuille d'herbe: elle est sur pied mais facilement se flétrit. L'époux comme une touffe d'algue qui pousse confinée sous l'eau et facilement se casse.

— Combien, jeune homme, avez-vous d'amantes?

— Moi, ma parente, je n'ai guère d'amantes, car elles ne sont que sept mes amantes: la première est l'amante qui me taille les ongles; la deuxième est l'amante qui remplace dehors celle qui est chez nous dans la maison; la troisième est l'amante qui la remplace dans les cas pressés; la quatrième est l'amante qui me suit longuement des yeux quand je pars; la cinquième est l'amante qui vient à ma rencontre quand je rentre; la sixième est l'amante qui sustente ma vie à l'égal du riz; la septième est l'amante qui ne mêle pas sa crasse avec celle de la foule et qui, quand bien même il lui arrive de s'y confondre sait toujours se distinguer.

*

– Can I come in? Can I come in?

– Who is it? Who is it?

– Me, the first-born of my father and my mother.

– The first-born of his father and mother, who has fine-coloured clothes and holds his head high? Who hops in his shoes, and then goes to rest in his palanquin? Well, come in then, young man. The little calf is safely tied up and my father and mother are far away. Still, if you want to see a cloth as fine as wings of a grasshopper or a dragonfly, you must go somewhere else. Or if you come for the brief regrets of love, I would rather send you off before I see you.

*

There in the north stand two stones and they are somewhat alike: one is black and the other is white. If I pick up the white one, the black one shames me. If I pick up the black one, the white one shames me. If I pick them both up, one is love, the other consolation.

*

A wife is like a blade of grass: she stands upright but easily wilts. A husband is like a tuft of seaweed growing confined beneath the water and is easily broken.

– Young man, how many sweethearts have you?

– My cousin, I have hardly any sweethearts, for my sweethearts are only seven: the first is the sweetheart who cuts my nails; the second is the sweetheart who takes the place of the one at home, when I am out of doors; the third takes her place in time of need; the fourth is the sweetheart who follows me lingeringly with her eyes when I go away; the fifth is the sweetheart who comes to meet me when I return; the sixth is the sweetheart who sustains my life as rice does; the seventh is the sweetheart who does not rub her dirt in the crowd's dirt and even when she happens to be amongst them always knows how to make herself distinguished.

*

– A-t-il enfin les ailes brisées, le Prince-libellule, à force de voler? Est-elle enfin mariée, la Belle-naïve, après un long célibat?

– La Belle-naïve n'est pas mariée après un long célibat. Ce n'est pas l'oiseau blanc qui marche en titubant que je méprise, ni le grand héron qui reste la bouche béante: je suis la Jeune-femme-qui-n'a-qu'une-parole, et je me garderai bien d'y ajouter du remords!

– Are his wings broken at last, the Dragonfly Prince, from so much flying? Is she married at last, the Ingenuous Fair, after so long a maidenhood?

– The Ingenuous Fair is not married after so long a maidenhood. It is not the white bird who staggers as he walks that I despise, nor the great heron that stands open-mouthed: I am the Young-woman-who-has-but-one-word and I'll take good care to keep that free from remorse.

DATE		